Computer Programmer

CAREERS WITH CHARACTER

Career Assessments and Their Meanings

Childcare Worker

Clergy

Computer Programmer

Financial Advisor

Firefighter

Homeland Security Officer

Journalist

Manager

Military and Elite Forces Officer

Nurse

Politician

Professional Athlete and Sports Official

Psychologist

Research Scientist

Social Worker

Special Education Teacher

Veterinarian

Careers with Character

Computer Programmer

by Sherry Bonnice

MASON CREST PUBLISHERS

Mason Crest Publishers Inc.
370 Reed Road
Broomall, Pennsylvania 19008
(866) MCP-BOOK (toll free)
www.masoncrest.com

First printing
1 2 3 4 5 6 7 8 9 10
Library of Congress Cataloging-in-Publication Data on file at the Library of Congress.
ISBN 1-59084-312-6
        1-59084-327-4 (series)

Design by Lori Holland.
Composition by Bytheway Publishing Services, Binghamton, New York.
Printed and bound in the Hashemite Kingdom of Jordan.

Photo Credits:
Comstock: pp. 26, 36, 38, 54, 65, 66, 72, 76
Corbis: pp. 13, 31, 32,
Digital Stock: pp. 29, 41, 56
PhotoDisc: pp. 4, 7, 8, 9, 11, 16, 18, 19, 20, 21, 28, 39, 40, 44, 46, 47, 48, 49, 58, 60, 62, 64, 67, 74, 75, 78, 80, 83, cover

Contents

Introduction   1

1. Job Requirements   5

2. Integrity and Trustworthiness   17

3. Respect and Compassion   27

4. Justice and Fairness   37

5. Responsibility   45

6. Courage   55

7. Self-Discipline and Diligence   63

8. Citizenship   73

9. Career Opportunities   79

Further Reading   86
For More Information   87
Glossary   88
Index   89

We each leave a fingerprint on the world.
Our careers are the work we do in life.
Our characters are shaped by the choices
we make to do good.
When we combine careers with character,
we touch the world with power.

INTRODUCTION

by Dr. Cheryl Gholar
and Dr. Ernestine G. Riggs

In today's world, the awesome task of choosing or staying in a career has become more involved than one would ever have imagined in past decades. Whether the job market is robust or the demand for workers is sluggish, the need for top-performing employees with good character remains a priority on most employers' lists of "must have" or "must keep." When critical decisions are being made regarding a company or organization's growth or future, job performance and work ethic are often the determining factors as to who will remain employed and who will not.

How does one achieve success in one's career and in life? Victor Frankl, the Austrian psychologist, summarized the concept of success in the preface to his book *Man's Search for Meaning* as: "The unintended side-effect of one's personal dedication to a course greater than oneself." Achieving value by responding to life and careers from higher levels of knowing and being is a specific goal of teaching and learning in "Careers with Character." What constitutes success for us as individuals can be found deep within our belief system. Seeking, preparing, and attaining an excellent career that aligns with our personality is an outstanding goal. However, an excellent career augmented by exemplary character is a visible expression of the human need to bring meaning, purpose, and value to our work.

Career education informs us of employment opportunities, occupational outlooks, earnings, and preparation needed to perform certain

1

tasks. Character education provides insight into how a person of good character might choose to respond, initiate an action, or perform specific tasks in the presence of an ethical dilemma. "Careers with Character" combines the two and teaches students that careers are more than just jobs. Career development is incomplete without character development. What better way to explore careers and character than to make them a single package to be opened, examined, and reflected upon as a means of understanding the greater whole of who we are and what work can mean when one chooses to become an employee of character?

Character can be defined simply as "who you are even when no one else is around." Your character is revealed by your choices and actions. These bear your personal signature, validating the story of who you are. They are the fingerprints you leave behind on the people you meet and know; they are the ideas you bring into reality. Your choices tell the world what you truly believe.

Character, when viewed as a standard of excellence, reminds us to ask ourselves when choosing a career: "Why this particular career, for what purpose, and to what end?" The authors of "Careers with Character" knowledgeably and passionately, through their various vignettes, enable one to experience an inner journey that is both intellectual and moral. Students will find themselves, when confronting decisions in real life, more prepared, having had experiential learning opportunities through this series. The books, however, do not separate or negate the individual good from the academic skills or intellect needed to perform the required tasks that lead to productive career development and personal fulfillment.

Each book is replete with exemplary role models, practical strategies, instructional tools, and applications. In each volume, individuals of character work toward ethical leadership, learning how to respond appropriately to issues of not only right versus wrong, but issues of right versus right, understanding the possible benefits and consequences of their decisions. A wealth of examples is provided.

What is it about a career that moves our hearts and minds toward fulfilling a dream? It is our character. The truest approach to finding out who we are and what illuminates our lives is to look within. At the very heart of career development is good character. At the heart of good character is an individual who knows and loves the good, and seeks to share the good with others. By exploring careers and character together, we create internal and external environments that support and enhance each other, challenging students to lead conscious lives of personal quality and true richness every day.

Is there a difference between doing the right thing, and doing things right? Career questions ask, "What do you know about a specific career?" Character questions ask, "Now that you know about a specific career, what will you choose to do with what you know?" "How will you perform certain tasks and services for others, even when no one else is around?" "Will all individuals be given your best regardless of their socioeconomic background, physical condition, ethnicity, or religious beliefs?" Character questions often challenge the authenticity of what we say we believe and value in the workplace and in our personal lives.

Character and career questions together challenge us to pay attention to our lives and not fall asleep on the job. Career knowledge, self-knowledge, and ethical wisdom help us answer deeper questions about the meaning of work; they give us permission to transform our lives. Personal integrity is the price of admission.

The insight of one "ordinary" individual can make a difference in the world—if that one individual believes that character is an amazing gift to uncap knowledge and talents to empower the human community. Our world needs everyday heroes in the workplace—and "Careers with Character" challenges students to become those heroes.

The world of computers demands skill and expertise—and the qualities of a good character.

1

JOB REQUIREMENTS

*Demonstrating positive character traits will
have an effect on your career.*

In 1981, when Linus Torvalds was 11 years old, his grandfather gave him his first computer. The Finnish youth worked in front of it endlessly. His own simple program using the **BASIC** programming language was the result of his diligence. Building on his first program success, Torvalds next wrote his first video game. Later, as a computer science student at the University of Helsinki, he purchased a 33-MHz 386 PC. Desiring more capability than was available on the **operating system** of this computer and unable to afford Unix, a larger, more powerful system, Torvald made a decision: he would develop and write his own operating system, a Unix **clone**. This was only the first of his decisions that would impact the international computer community for many years.

As Torvalds developed the new operating system **kernel**, he shared his struggles with other programmers, via the Internet. In 1991, when Torvalds was 22 years old, the completed source code came to be known as Linux (pronounced "lin-ucks") in his honor. With Linux ready for use, he made another major decision: he posted the code for free on the Internet. This generous decision still allows anyone anywhere in the world to work with and improve on the system and then share it with the rest of the programming community. In essence, he created an environment where thousands of programmers could work together to better the system.

Many young people today are interested in computers; their interest often leads them to spend long hours experimenting with computers—and this experience builds a solid base of knowledge. If you are interested in a career in computer programming, you can begin learning as a young person, just as Torvalds did.

Although almost anyone with a computer and enough interest can become knowledgeable in computer programming, most employers look for a bachelor's degree or higher in computer science, mathematics, or information systems. However, a person who has a degree in accounting, inventory control, or other areas of business may supplement their studies with special computer programming courses. Some specialized fields require graduate degrees.

Programmers today still enjoy the use of programs like Linux, but most programmers are hired to develop and write programs specific to the needs of their employers. The educational background varies for

The Principles of Good Character

1. Your character is defined by what you do, not what you say or believe.
2. Every choice you make helps define the kind of person you are choosing to be.
3. Good character requires doing the right thing, even when it is costly or risky.
4. You don't have to take the worst behavior of others as a standard for yourself. You can choose to be better than that.
5. What you do matters, and one person can make an important difference.
6. The payoff for good character is that it makes you a better person and it makes the world a better place.

Adapted from www.goodcharacter.com

Programming languages like COBOL and Prolog are the building blocks for the computer programs that run your computer.

those involved in financial programming and those who write games for the ever-growing software market. Once a program is designed, a programmer must transform it into steps, one by one. The computer must be told each operation in a logical order. These instructions are written in code using **a *programming language*** such as ***COBOL*** or ***Prolog***. Once written, a program must be tested. Changing and rechecking errors may mean long hours, nights, and possibly weekends of work. Just like Torvalds, who kept the copyright to Linux so that he would be sure each new version was tested before release, programmers can pride themselves in the integrity of their written code.

Systems programmers write programs that maintain and control computer software. They work on operating systems, like Linux. They also work on network systems and database systems. When programmers write programs that carry out a specific job, they are called applications programmers. They devise billing systems or track inventory. They may revise existing software to better fit the needs of their employers.

One of the largest growing markets in the computer industry is software development. Creating packaged software can range from games to educational software to spreadsheets. Most computer programmers are employed by the computer and data processing services industry, which includes those who write and sell software.

The First Computer

The first computer, built in 1946, had dimensions of 3 feet by 8 feet by 100 feet, and it weighed 30 tons.

Programmers working in many different fields will have access to confidential information. Very often, facts about the company or its clients are essential to the writing of code. Government programmers also have access to information that could affect national security. Because of the magnitude and far-reaching consequences of the September 11, 2001 crisis, national security will be an important issue for anyone who works in key government positions.

Issues like these mean that in the field of computer programming,

Today's computers are small enough to fit on a desk—or carry in a brief case. Early computers were enormous by comparison.

Computer whizzes have the opportunity to hack into private computers—and they also have the chance to make a positive difference in the world. Each individual must choose for himself which path to take.

knowledge alone is not enough. Many individuals in our world today choose to use their computer savvy in negative ways. They **hack** into private computers to steal information or gain access to bank accounts; they develop destructive **viruses** that can cost our society millions of dollars. The bad reputation of computer "whizzes" like these makes employers cautious; they are seeking programmers who possess sterling characters.

As the president of the Character Counts Coalition, Michael Josephson teaches that character makes an important difference in

Transmission Control Protocol/ Internet Protocol

Until 1983 there was no common language for all computers to use to communicate with each other. Robert Kahn and Vinton Cerf invented the standard Internet language called TCP/IP, Transmission Control Protocol/Internet Protocol. This invention made possible the Internet so many of us use and enjoy today.

our lives and the lives of those with whom we come in contact. *Choosing* to be an employee who embodies core values allows us to demonstrate these qualities in the workplace and to treat others as we would like to be treated ourselves. When we show respect, the chances of receiving respect are much greater. The same happens as we share any of the core character traits.

A Computer Programmer

When Mark Andreesen was about eight, he taught himself the Basic programming language by reading a book borrowed from a local library. He wrote his first program in the sixth grade, using a personal computer in his school's library. The program was designed to help him with his math homework.

In high school, he created a matchmaking program for classmates searching for dates. By the time he was in college, he was working as a part-time computer programmer in 1992 at the University of Illinois' National Center for Supercomputing Applicatons (NCSA). He talked Eric Bina, a fellow employee at NCSA, into working together to create an Internet browser. Bringing on a team of people, they created a prototype called NCSA Mosaic that featured point-and-click navigation.

After he earned his bachelor's degree in computer science from the University of Illinois at Urbab-Champaign in 1993, he interned with IBM in Austin, Texas. Millionaire James Clark, founder of Silicon Graphics, e-mailed Andreesen about forming a new company. With $4 million of Clark's money, they started Mosaic Communications in April 1994. They changed the name to Netscape Communications in November 1994.

You never know what may happen when you enter the field of computer programming!

Computer programs are used in many settings, including schools.

Supreme Court Justice Clarence Thomas's views
on character. . .

. . . I wonder if we are not allowing ourselves to point
fingers at others rather than look to ourselves for
solutions. I often ask myself whether I am content to see
the problem in my neighbor rather than in myself.

For example, a person of character is a pillar of his
family and community and, I might add, leads by
example.

. . . Our character does not require extraordinary
intelligence, a privileged upbringing, or significant
wealth. Nor, for that matter, is character a matter of
accomplishing extraordinary feats or undertaking
magnanimous acts. Looking back on the lives of my
grandparents—who were barely able to read and saddled
with the burdens of segregation—I have come to realize
that people of every station in life can influence the world
in which we live. But for them, where would my brother
and I be? It is the small things we do each day, the often
mundane and routine tasks, that form our habits and
seem to have the most lasting impression on our fellow
man. We have it within us to influence the many lives we
do and should touch every day, including our own lives.

"Does character matter?" the answer is emphatically
"Yes. Character is all that matters."

Adapted from material from www.heritage.org/heritage25/lectures/feb98/
thomas.html.

In the chapters that follow we will look at the following character traits in more detail:

- Integrity and trustworthiness
- Respect and compassion
- Justice and fairness
- Responsibility
- Courage
- Self-discipline and diligence
- Citizenship

"Controlling our attitudes is not easy," Josephson admits. "It takes character to harness powerful and instinctive feelings and redirect

Canada Promotes Computers and Their Value to Future Employment

On October 15, 1998 in Toronto, Ontario, John Manley, Canadian Minister of Industry, launched Canada's SchoolNet GrassRoots National Campaign. Working with the provinces and territories, the SchoolNet GrassRoots program wants to encourage Canadian K–12 teachers and students to develop on-line learning projects in the classroom. The hope is that students will then be better prepared academically and technologically for employment.

Today's medical technology depends on computer programs.

our thoughts toward positive attitudes, but those who do live happier lives in a happier world."

Working as a computer programmer who demonstrates these qualities will make a difference in our world.

The happiness of your life depends on the quality of your thoughts: therefore, guard accordingly, and take care that you entertain no notions unsuitable to virtue and reasonable nature.

—Marcus Aurelius

Computer programmers have a fascinating job with the potential for financial gain. Character issues like integrity and trustworthiness, however, are easily lost amid the work's pressures.

2

INTEGRITY AND
TRUSTWORTHINESS

*Choosing the right path may be especially
difficult if another person experiences
consequences because of your choice.*

Matt Franklin and his business partner Kim Lee won their first area
government contract when they were hired to set up an interactive web site for the county commissioners. Bidding against four other
firms, Matt and Kim felt they had submitted a fair price for the required
needs of the county officials; the county government agreed, and Matt
and Kim got the job. Their fees were fixed, which meant rather than receiving an hourly rate, they would get only a flat price for the setup and
one year of maintenance. Keeping their labor on schedule would be important to assure that the job was profitable.

The site would allow constituents to answer questions about issues
so that the commissioners received a more immediate and efficient way
to assess local opinion. Matt and Kim met a few times with the commissioners to ask questions and plan the site. Once they had gathered
the necessary data, Matt felt secure about the project. He and Kim
would now work at choosing font types, finding or designing appropriate art and pictures, and being sure that everything linked together
properly on the pages. If the site did not load quickly or if it was not

easy to navigate, people would be less likely to use it. In their proposal they had assured their client they would provide an inviting site that could be updated easily.

Kim wrote the code while Matt tested each piece to be sure it worked as they had planned. Once the individual coding for each section was interfaced together, they examined the site. Everything looked great. The site was easy to access, moving from page to page was quick, and recording information requested by the commissioners was straightforward. Finally, Matt checked over the code for any last-minute problems before he and Kim presented the project to the commissioners.

A Definition

Integrity *noun:* Steadfast adherence to a strict moral or ethical code.

As Matt examined the program code, he noticed that besides being easy to use on the site, it was also easy to change in the code language. Because they would need to maintain the site regularly, Kim had con-

Computer programmers often work in teams.

When two people work together, open communication is a necessary part of working with integrity.

structed it so it could be easily modified, convenient for him and Matt. Unfortunately, this was also an aspect that could be used by anyone who might want to alter data, something the commissioners wanted definitely to avoid. The site had to be private and secure. The local government wanted honest answers from the voters so the commissioners could better serve their constituents' real needs. And the commissioners wanted those answers to be tamper-free.

Matt did not know what to do. If he complained to Kim, it would mean hours of work rewriting code that worked but was not secure. The extra hours of rewriting would mean a monetary loss for both of them; they had already agreed on a price, and they couldn't go back now and ask for more money. But if they left the code as it was, someone might discover how to alter the voters' answers. If the ease with which changes could be made was found out by the local government, Matt and Kim might lose the contract altogether. But of course this would only be a problem if someone realized how easily they could change the answers.

Are You a Person of Integrity?

(Take this self-evaluation and find out. Answer yes or no.)

1. I always try to do what is right, even when it's costly or difficult.
2. I am truthful, sincere, and straightforward.
3. I don't lie, cheat, or steal.
4. I don't intentionally mislead others.
5. I don't compromise my values by giving in to temptation.

Your integrity is your gift to yourself and to the world.

Adapted from Character Education at www.goodcharacter.com

Life offers no delete button—so character decisions need to be made carefully.

Life is full of balancing acts—and balancing integrity and profit margin is no easy task.

What should Matt do? Was it more important to make a higher profit margin on their work? After all, maybe no one would ever notice how easy the program was to enter and change. Or should he and Kim present a product of which they were 100 percent proud, one that worked as it was intended for their clients?

According to the Josephson Institute of Ethics, any decision affecting other people has ethical implications—and trustworthiness is one of the core ethical principles. Using the principles offered by the Josephson Institute to make his decision, Matt needed to:

1. *Realize and eliminate his unethical options*, those things he perceived as wrong. Ethical commitment means doing the right thing, especially when doing so imposes financial, social, or emotional costs. Ethical people need the fortitude to follow their conscience. Even though Matt and Kim might have to pay a price for the right decision, they must choose between what they want and what they want to *be*.

CHEATING
True or False Quiz

1. Everyone's doing it.
   False. Though cheating is rampant, polls shows that somewhere between 20 and 40 percent of students don't cheat.
2. When you cheat, you only cheat yourself.
   False. You also cheat others—like friends who do the work; you cheat your family, your teachers, and anyone who trusts you.
3. Academic pressure is a poor excuse for cheating.
   True. While today's students do feel pressured to perform well, those who don't cheat still get good grades and are accepted by excellent colleges.
4. If you cheat once, it's not likely you'll make a habit of it.
   False. Cheating is like an addiction. You always think you will only do it once but usually once is never the end of a bad habit.

Adapted from *TEEN*, Aug. 1998, pp. 96+

2. *Admit that he wanted to be trusted*, both in the workplace and in his personal life. Matt would be working with people he knew. Some of his colleagues, as well as some personal friends, would visit the site when they felt a need to contact the county commissioners. Matt realized he wanted others—his friends, acquaintances, and even people he had never met—to consider him trustworthy.

3. *Recognize that the feelings of doubt and questioning meant he knew it was wrong to not give the best he had to offer.* He would want the same from someone who worked for him. He wanted it from his children . . . and he certainly expected it from himself.

4. *Confront Kim with the problem* and assure him that he understood why Kim had written the code the way he had—but that it would be a security problem they could not afford. Matt did not look forward to confronting Kim, but Matt knew if he were the one who had made a mistake of this magnitude, he would want Kim to bring it to his attention.

5. *Reevaluate how they will bid on future projects.* The code needing some alterations might not be the whole problem. Maybe he and Kim needed to look at how they bid on jobs, how they figured in labor time, and if they included enough margin for error. Certainly he and Kim needed to expect that things could and would go wrong with each project they were involved in programming. Setting up a better bidding system might save them a lot of trouble in the future. Matt also knew they needed to realize that a local govern-

> Integrity is not about getting what we want; it's about being what we want. It's not about winning; it's about staying whole and being worthy of self-respect and the esteem of loved ones. It's about being honorable, not as a success strategy, but a life choice.
> —Michael Josephson

> **To Be a Person of Integrity**
>
> Tell the truth.
> Keep your word.
> Do what you say you will do.
> Be honest with yourself.
> Do right even when no one else is looking.

> He who permits himself to tell a lie once finds it much easier to do it a second time, till at length it becomes habitual. He tells lies without attending to it, and truths without the world's believing him. This falsehood of the tongue leads to that of the heart, and in time depraves all its good dispositions.
> —Thomas Jefferson

ment job could open up many other doors for them. Future work might override some loss in their profit margin for this job.

Using these principles, what actions do you think Matt will take next? What would you do in his place?

Speak with integrity.
Say only what you mean.
Avoid using the word to speak against yourself or to gossip
  about others.
Use the power of your word in the direction of truth and love.

—Don Miguel Ruiz

When computer programmers work together, their relationship can be as competitive as a duel—or they can work together with respect and compassion for one another.

3

RESPECT AND COMPASSION

Sometimes it takes effort to look beneath
the surface of a problem to find the real
obstacle to your success.

D on't worry so much."

Manny sighed. "Pete, without your test results, I can't go on with the project. My deadline is next Tuesday. I need time to work on your data."

Pete shook his head and laughed. "Man, you gotta relax a little. You'll have lots of time."

Manny walked back to his desk. He and Pete were updating the billing system for their company; the project had been assigned over a month ago. Normally, they each worked on a separate object file, and later the files were put together and tested by the project manager. This time, though, the project manager was on vacation, so Manny was responsible for interfacing the billing code and testing to be sure there were no problems in the system before the Tuesday deadline.

Although Manny felt he and Pete shared a friendship as well as a working relationship, since the beginning of the project Manny had noticed a change in Pete. Something seemed to be wrong. Pete's attitude was abrupt and he avoided talking about the job and its problems with Manny. Working on job-related questions was something they used to do often to help each other through any programming issues that had them stumped. Now Pete always seemed to have a fast, flip answer that brought an end to any conversation. When they were away from their desks, things were no better. Pete didn't even want to discuss baseball anymore.

Another day passed and Manny still did not receive any code from Pete. An E-mail he sent to Pete was left unanswered all day. Manny needed to do something. He was frustrated and worried and a little angry—but he wanted to try one more time to persuade Pete to share what was going on with him. Manny decided on a new approach.

"Hey, Pete, how's it going?"

"No, it's not ready, Manny. Can't you see I'm working?"

"How about if I look at the program with you? Maybe we can go through some of the coding together," Manny offered.

Some Definitions

Respect *noun:* Consideration.
Compassion *noun:* Deep awareness of the suffering of another coupled with the wish to relieve it.

A good programmer not only needs computer skills—he also needs the ability to get along well with his coworkers.

Ethical decisions often arise during conversations with others. The character qualities of respect and compassion can help guide us through those dilemmas.

"What? Don't you think I can handle it myself?" Pete slammed his file drawer shut. Manny got the feeling Pete was trying to hide something.

"Come on, Pete. I'm just trying to help. Where's the problem? Is there some part of the program that's not working right? Is there a problem with the client's data?"

"No. There's no problem with anything. I just need time to get it done, okay, Manny? I'll have it done. Let me get back to work."

When Manny left Pete's office, he felt worse than ever. He had to get that data so he could check for any interface problems with his own data.

> An ethical dilemma is a situation where we must make a choice about what is right . . . and what is wrong.

Pete was a good programmer. Manny knew this because they had worked together on other projects. This was not a very difficult project, but they did need to be sure the parts worked together and

A Framework for Ethical Decision Making

People of character keep in mind the concerns of others. When confronted with an ethical dilemma, these are some questions we might ask:

- Is there something wrong personally, interpersonally, or socially?
- What are the relevant facts of the case?
- What individuals and groups have an important stake in the outcome? What is at stake for each? Do some have a greater stake because they have a special need (for example, those who are poor or excluded) or because we have special obligations to them?
- What are the options for acting?
- Which option will produce the most good and do the least harm?
- Which option would enable the deepening or development of those virtues or character traits that we value as individuals? As a profession? As a society?

Adapted from materials from the Markkula Center for Applied Ethics, Santa Clara University, 500 El Camino Real, Santa Clara, CA 95053-0633.

that the product was sound before releasing it to management. Pete needed to retrieve the original data from the client and begin the coding.

Manny hated to go to his boss. He knew that would mean Pete would have a full review; he might then be put on probation for six months and all his work would be monitored not only by their project manager but also by upper management. It would mean extra reports and meetings for Pete during the whole period. Manny hated to put his friend through that if there was another alternative. But what should he do?

Respect and compassion ask that we give the other person a chance to explain his point of view.

After considering his options, Manny decided he would look at the problem from Pete's point of view. If he were Pete, what would he be thinking and doing? He knew Pete was aware of the Tuesday deadline and that Pete had met every other deadline while he and Manny had worked together. Pete also knew that Manny had come to him often when he was having a code problem; in fact, they shared many such problems with each other and had worked them through together on other occasions. Things were good for Pete at home as far as Manny knew; in fact, just yesterday Manny had run into Pete's wife Jill at the grocery store and she had com-

> ### If I Can Stop One Heart From Breaking
>
> If I can stop one heart from
> breaking,
> I shall not live in vain;
> If I can ease one life the aching,
> Or cool one pain,
> Or help one fainting robin
> Unto his nest again,
> I shall not live in vain.
> —Emily Dickinson
> (1830–1886)

Computer programmers, like many other workers, must communicate frequently with others by phone and in person. Good communications skills make their job go more smoothly.

mented on what a good summer their entire family was having. She had looked genuinely happy with life, and Manny had a feeling Pete's home life wasn't the source of his problems. That only left the clients' data. Could that be the problem?

Acting in his temporary role as project manager, Manny made a few phone calls. After being transferred from one representative to another, he discovered the problem at last: the data had not been sent to Pete. The problem was not Pete but the clients. They had not kept their part of the contract. But why hadn't Pete told Manny right from the start?

"Hey, Pete." Manny smiled as he walked into his friend's office.

"Yeah, I know what you're go-

> If you can learn a simple trick . . . you'll get along a lot better with all kinds of folks. You never really understand a person until you consider things from his point of view . . . until you climb into his skin and walk around in it.
>
> —Atticus Finch speaking to his daughter in *To Kill a Mockingbird* by Harper Lee

Code Analyzers

Programmers must write the most efficient programs possible. In order to do this, programs must contain the least memory and storage space possible. But they also must run at fast speeds.

To help with optimizing programs, special analyzing programs have been developed to examine the source code. With this information the programmer makes the program run faster.

ing to say. Is my part of the program ready yet?" Pete pushed his chair back from his desk and ran his fingers through his hair. He looked tired and worried.

"No, I just wanted to tell you I know you don't have the data yet."

"How do you know that?" Pete asked.

"Well, I couldn't figure out what was wrong. I knew it wasn't like you to hold up a project. So I made some phone calls. Why didn't you just tell me?"

Pete sighed. "I just felt like it was my job, my problem. I can't keep coming running to you to bail me out every time I run into something. I can take care of myself. Besides, I didn't want to ask you to stick your neck out just because we're friends. I mean work is work."

"Hey, we're working on this together. I'm not bailing you out—we just need to figure some other way to get the clients moving. Besides, if I can't stick my neck out for my friend, than who can I stick it out for? Let's see what we can do next."

Manny might just as easily have gone to his boss and gotten the solution he wanted. But because he cared for Pete and relied on the experiences he had had in the past with him, Manny and Pete were able to work together on a solution to their problem. If Manny had not taken time to put himself in Pete's shoes, however, he might never have discovered the problem until it was too late to solve.

When confronted with an ethical dilemma, a person needs to ask several questions. In order to define the moral issue, he or she can ask if something is wrong personally, interpersonally, or socially. In order to get the facts, he or she can ask, What are the options for acting? Have all the relevant persons and groups been consulted? These are the same questions Manny asked himself when making his decision about Pete. If he had not taken the time to understand Pete's position, the consequences for Pete could have been far reaching.

Can you apply these same questions to any dilemma you face in your life?

Respect your fellow human beings, treat them fairly, disagree with them honestly, enjoy their friendship, explore your thoughts about one another candidly, work together for a common goal and help one another achieve it.

—Bill Bradley

Justice and fairness ask that we not shove others out of our way in our race to success.

4

JUSTICE AND FAIRNESS

*When you work closely with others on a
project, care must be taken that everyone's
work and ideas are represented fairly.*

Andrea Landis began her career working at one of the large area
banks. As a programmer on a team of four, she learned quickly
with the help of her teammates. Many of their projects were enhanced
because they shared concepts and ideas. Andrea worked well with the
group and they excelled because of their cooperative spirit.

In the early 1990s, after Andrea had worked three years with the
team, management assigned the team a project to **automate** checking
accounts. As the team members shared ideas with one another, Tracey
Allen mentioned the possibility of allowing customers to write checks
at the Internet site. They could go to the site to pay bills or transfer
funds. Besides being able to perform these tasks electronically, they
could work around their own schedules, not just banking hours. None
of the competing banks were offering the service yet. Dan Yoder and
Joe Karban agreed that it would be a cutting-edge service. But as the
team began work to fulfill the objectives outlined for them by management, they decided to move in a different direction and the idea for on-
line checking was dropped along the way.

After work that night, however, Andrea found herself thinking
again about the possibility of writing checks on-line. It really was a

great idea. As a customer, she would love to be able to eliminate some of the work involved in monthly bill paying. She knew the vice president of customer services, Jim Finch, would love the idea; he was very progressive, always looking for new ways to accommodate their customers. The next day, Andrea decided, she would bring up the idea again at the team project meeting. They really needed to reconsider the idea; Andrea thought they had been a little too hasty in setting it aside.

Of course, Andrea knew all too well the major problem faced by most programmers—deadlines. The automated checking project

Some Definitions

Justice *noun:* Conformity to moral rightness in action or attitude; righteousness; taking personal responsibility to uphold what is pure, right, and true.
Fairness *noun:* Practicing justice, equity, and equality. Cooperating with one another. Recognizing the uniqueness and value of each individual within our diverse society.

Computer programming has transformed the world of banking.

Deadlines add pressure to a computer programmer's work.

had been put on rush by management and the outlined objectives would take considerable time already. But she was sure if they looked at the advantages of on-line banking, the team would agree that it was worth including this as part of their automated checking. Tracey had had a really good idea. Jim would surely extend the deadline if a major change were necessary to improve the project.

Andrea arrived at work earlier than usual the next morning. As she poured a cup of tea, she met Jim, the vice president getting himself a cup of coffee.

Jim took a sip of his coffee. "How's the project coming?"

> ### A Personal Vow of Justice
>
> I will. . .
>
> 1. Obey the law.
> 2. Speak out for what is pure, right, and true.
> 3. Never prejudge others.
> 4. Always remain open to reason.
> 5. Keep my conscience clean.
>
> Adapted from material from the Baton Rouge Character First Program, 222 St. Louis Street, Rm. 936, Baton Rouge, LA 70802.

"Good. We've got a firm start and hope to stay right on schedule."

Jim looked pleased. "This is a great opportunity to improve customer relations. We ought to be able to answer account questions more quickly and get necessary information to customers in about half the time."

"I agree. You know I was thinking last night about the possibility of writing checks on-line. It would give more flexibility to the customer and it hasn't been done in this area yet."

"Writing checks on line." Jim's thoughtful look changed to one of excitement. "That's it! Exactly what we're looking for in our automated checking program. Perfect, Andrea, we'll do it."

Jim met with the team that morning. After discussing what needed to be done to include on-line checking in the services the bank offered, he decided to move back the team's deadline for the automated checking project. Each programmer received an assignment, and the project became a great source of pride for the team, the bank, and Jim.

Not long after the project was operating, Jim called Andrea to his

Most computer programmers don't work in isolation; team meetings are a part of many workdays.

On-line checking—made possible by computer programmers—allows bankers to save time and no longer write checks by hand.

office. "Great job coming up with that idea. On-line checking is a major success. Customers love the convenience and the board of directors loves when customers are happy." Jim laughed.

"I've heard some positive comments myself," Andrea agreed.

"Since it was your idea that got us going on the right track, I wanted to share an opportunity with you. Recently, one of our employees moved out of the area, leaving an opening in development. I'm wondering if you would like the position. Of course, it comes with a substantial salary increase."

Andrea was taken by surprise. "Well, thanks, Jim but. . ."

"Think about it before you answer. It will mean some changes, but this is a great opportunity for you. And we're looking for someone who's not afraid to pursue new ideas."

This was exactly the promotion Andrea had hoped to receive. Working in development, she would have the chance to evaluate the needs of both the customer and the company; she could use her creative skills to make suggestions for improvements and incorporate changes in the bank's computer programming. She would be more connected to people, just what she wanted. Andrea was so excited she could hardly wait to share the news.

Then she remembered the original planning meeting. Tracey had been the one who made the suggestion to include on-line checking in their automated banking services. Andrea had shared Tracey's idea with Jim—but she hadn't thought of it herself.

What should Andrea do now? If the promotion had been offered to her because of the idea, then it was really Tracey's promotion, wasn't it? Should Andrea tell Jim the truth? Should she recommend Tracey for the position instead? Would anyone ever find out if she simply took the position and kept quiet?

Andrea knew she had an important decision to make. She thought about seeking advice from a good friend . . . but she wanted to reason out the problem herself. Her conscience, her internal barometer of right and wrong, was already hard at work.

Andrea knew that she had to look at the problem from her point of view—but also from Tracey's. If she were going to act fairly, she had to treat Tracey as she would want to be treated herself. She had to consider the effects of her decision on Tracey. And she needed to determine what was the fair and just thing to do.

Andrea asked herself these questions as she prepared to make the decision:

What would I think if I found out that Tracey had gotten a promotion and a raise because of an idea that had been my original idea?

What would the other members of the team think if they find out?

If I take the promotion, how will I feel five years from now? Will I feel guilty? Will I feel I cheated and lied to get ahead?

What about my children? How would I feel if they found out what choice I made? Could I face them and be proud of my decision?

What do you think Andrea should do? What would you do if you were in her place?

Injustice anywhere is a threat to justice everywhere.

—Martin Luther King, Jr.

As a high school student, choosing career responsibilities is not easy—and throughout life new dilemmas will present themselves.

5

RESPONSIBILITY

*When we are responsible to our vocation,
friends, and family, we sometimes encounter
situations where our obligations conflict.*

During Ken Maines' college internship, he was grateful for the opportunity to work as a programmer on a government project in Washington, D.C. Computer programming had not been his original career plan—a job as an FBI or CIA agent had always been his dream—but he knew he was fortunate to have found an alternate profession that came very close to his lifelong ambition. He knew the promising position and his responsibility to the agency that employed him was a privilege.

Since he was a teenager, Ken had always longed to work in a top secret environment. He loved spy movies and books and often imagined himself in dangerous situations. He also loved to travel and wanted to learn more about other cultures. He was sure a James Bond assignment was in his future.

But during his junior year of high school, Ken was in a major automobile accident. His right leg was broken in three places, and even after two major surgeries he walked with a slight limp. Ken's math teacher, Mr. Derry, knew of some of Ken's aspirations to work in a secret service position. Realizing that fieldwork would not be a possibility now, Stephen Derry introduced Ken to another avenue of work that would help him achieve his dream in a different way.

An accident or physical disability can make our career path turn in a new direction.

After the accident, Mr. Derry volunteered to help Ken get around the school when he returned in a wheelchair. Before long, Ken was using crutches to navigate the halls, but by then the teacher and student had become good friends. But the most important thing Mr. Derry did for Ken was to introduce him to the world of computer programming.

Math and logic came easily to Ken, and he learned the computer languages quickly. Ken spent many after-school hours in Stephen Derry's computer lab, learning computer languages and programming skills; he and Mr. Derry discussed what Ken could do with his new knowledge. Ken had always connected computer programming with business jobs, but Mr. Derry helped him see the many and varied possibilities in this career.

> **A Definition**
>
> **Responsibility** *noun:*
> Something for which one is
> responsible; a duty or obligation.

In college, Ken studied programming and communications. He

Teachers and other adults can offer help and encouragement as you make career choices.

Many computer programmers find work in America's capital.

excelled in academics and made a name for himself in organizations on campus. All of his work had paid off now that he had received the government internship he had applied for.

Working in Washington was hard but worth every minute. Ken completed his internship and finished his senior year. After graduating, he realized his dream when he was offered a government position as a computer programmer.

When Ken agreed to work in top secret intelligence, he had to acquire clearances, including a thorough background investigation; credit and arrest checks; interviews with associates, employers, and neighbors; and verification of

Responsible Individuals:

1. Accept the consequences of their actions.
2. Perform their best.
3. Keep their commitments to friends, family, community, and country—and find a balance when these commitments conflict.
4. Don't make excuses or blame others for problems.

Computers Investigate

Computer systems help investigators searching for clues find some answers. For instance, computer programmers have designed programs that can match missing persons to unidentified bodies. Information about the physical descriptors, any pathological information, and anthropologic findings can be entered into the database. Systems like this can be used for missing persons or in mass disaster situations.

Forensic dentists, pathologists, coroners, medical examiners, forensic anthropologists, and law enforcement agents use programs written by computer programmers that search for all sorts of data about individuals to bring together the needed information. Many times the program gives the answers needed and the search ends.

The federal government employs computer programmers in the field of forensics.

his educational achievements. A drug test and polygraph examination were required. He also agreed to certain travel restrictions; some countries were classified by his agency as being hostile, and Ken would not be allowed to travel there because of his knowledge of sensitive information. Some of the agency's restrictions would affect his personal life as well, but he did not anticipate any serious difficulties.

Until his sister left on an exchange program for college, Ken's restricted travel was not a problem. But when Margaret decided to marry and live in South America, he was no longer as comfortable with his commitments to his employer.

Margaret and Pablo wanted to get married in the town where they would live, where Pablo had lived all his life. When Ken began to make arrangements to go to the wedding, his clearances immediately became an issue. He was not permitted to travel in the country where the wedding would take place, where his sister had chosen to make her new home. For the first time, he questioned his commitment to his job. He knew the reasons behind the restrictions against travel, but he just wasn't sure if they were over-exaggerated in this case.

Still, when he took his job, he had made a promise not to travel to restricted areas of the world. He felt responsible, not only to his job but also to his country. He had never expected to be in such a position—but now he was, and he had to make a choice. Did he owe his allegiance to his only sister—or his employer and country?

Doing the right thing had always come easily to him before. Now, however, he realized that right thing sometimes carries an expensive price. Before, he always assumed that as long as you did the right thing in life, you would win. For the first time, he realized that doing the ethical thing might have disagreeable consequences.

Ken decided that his responsibility to his job and to his country had to come first, even before his responsibility to his sister. The decision was not an easy one for him to make, and his sister and the rest of his family were not happy with him as a result of it. But he felt he was doing the right thing, the responsible thing, by not visiting his sister's new country. A few months after the wedding, Ken, his sister Margaret, and

Basic Moral Responsibilities

Dr. Thomas Lickona believes that because civilizations decline when individuals' lose their moral core, a basic responsibility adults have is to pass on the values that are the foundation of our society. Character education is the effort to plant and nurture good human qualities in the individual person and therefore the whole society. Such endeavors must be the result of great and diligent effort.

Children are most likely to become persons of character when they grow up in communities of character, where there is an effort on the part of families, schools, churches, temples, mosques, the media, the government, sports leagues, and all others who influence them to both model and teach these character qualities. That is a huge responsibility.

Historically, three institutions have shared character formation of the young: home, religion, and school. The family lays the foundation, which gets built upon by the other institutions. Adults need to come together to maximize the chance that we'll have a generation of young people who are mature enough and good enough to build the same ideals for the next generation. A partnership while raising children is very important. The Character Education Partnership, the leading national organization promoting character education, is called that precisely to convey a very clear message that it is not the job of schools, families, or religious institutions alone. We must all work together.

Do you feel responsible for modeling the qualities of a good character to those who are younger than you? Do you act on that responsibility?

Adapted from an interview hosted by *Early Childhood Today* with Thomas Lickona, Ph.D.

her new husband were able to spend a week of vacation together in the country bordering Margaret's new home—a country Ken was allowed to visit.

What would you have done? In Ken's place, you might have made another decision; for you, your responsibility to your family might have come first. In that case, however, you would have to deal with the consequences on another front: your job. You might very well face disciplinary action or even lose a job you love.

Getting what you want all the time can't be your goal if you want to do what is right. Instead, your long-term objective will be acting out the core qualities of a good character—like responsibility. The consequences may be painful sometimes, but no matter what others think, you can be proud of yourself.

I believe that every right implies a responsibility; every opportunity, an obligation; every possession, a duty.

—John D. Rockefeller, Jr.

As you climb the professional ladder to success, have the courage to stay true to your principles.

6

COURAGE

Sometimes courage means you do what's right . . . even when you don't like the consequences of your action.

Hiring Starkweathers, an independent firm, to make recommendations for the information management upgrades intimidated Brenda Pierce. She had worked on other projects with an outside team recommending changes and equipping the programmers with information, but this firm was known for its aggressiveness. She hoped she and her team would be able to execute the changes and fully integrate them into the existing system without having to defend or fight for those things her team knew were best for their company.

Brenda headed the company-based team gathered by the company president, Clark Seymour. Clark had worked hard to get backing from the board of directors, and he had taken a special interest in the upgrades. Once Starkweathers began studying the system, Brenda's team would match the details of their studies to the objectives. The two teams would work closely, allowing Starkweathers' firm access to the top programmers. The advantage to the company programmers would be the experience of a company who had met these same goals with other clients.

One of Brenda's favorite members of her team was Joe Franzoni who specialized in accounting. Joe always had something to say about

Computer programmers may need the courage to work out difficult decisions.

everything and his responses kept the team laughing. He had a talent for lightening up stressful situations. He wasn't just a clown, though; he was also sharp at his job. Several times, Brenda had seen him find a coding problem that others had missed.

"Something's wrong, Brenda," Joe said one day while they were working on some communication between company divisions.

"Wrong with what?"

Joe handed her a memo from accounting. Brenda read it and then looked up, a question in her eyes. "It's the automated delivery system. The system works to coordinate the buyers and sellers with the suppliers and customers. Another team is working on the project, and the internal accounting program will be changed once it is complete. So

> ### A Definition
>
> **Courage** *noun:* The state or quality of mind or spirit that enables one to face danger, fear, or change with self-possession, confidence, and resolution; bravery.

what's this got to do with us? It's someone else's baby, not ours."

"Do you realize that once this change is made, the entire system will be changed? So if we set up this program with what is here right now, it will be obsolete once the new accounting program begins operating."

> We gain strength, and courage, and confidence by each experience in which we really stop to look fear in the face . . . we must do that which we think we cannot.
> —Eleanor Roosevelt

"Whoa." Brenda frowned. "This is a major problem. Clark is not going to be happy."

"You're right about that. He loves this project. Brenda, you're the head of our team. What are you going to do?"

"I don't know. You're sure there are no other alternatives?"

Joe shook his head. "It's all said and done. I remember now. The other team started work before us, but I guess no one ever thought of the effect each project would have on the other. I think we're looking at

When it comes to ethical dilemmas, others may give you advice, but ultimately only you alone can reach an answer that's right for you.

Computer programs have financial effects that span the globe.

a million dollars for this project, and then another million and a half or more to disrupt it and make the change."

"So what we're looking at is a million-dollar project that if it goes into service as scheduled will probably need another million and a half or so to get everything interfaced with the new program for automated delivery." Brenda sighed. "This is scary."

The Olympic Creed

"The most important thing is not to win but to take part, just as the most important thing in life is not the triumph, but the struggle. The essential thing is not to have conquered, but to have fought well."

"Want me to call you in sick tomorrow?" Joe asked with a smile.

"No, I guess I have to find the courage to talk with Clark tomorrow morning. It has to be done before we put any more time into this project."

"Better you than me."

The following morning, Brenda left the vice president's office with an even larger problem. Clark re-

Why Is a Good Character Important?

It takes courage to live out all the other character qualities (like integrity, compassion, and responsibility). But why should we bother? Just so we can pat ourselves on the back and say what good people we are?

According to Thomas Lickona, our society benefits as a whole when individuals are courageous enough to stand up for what is right. The qualities of a good character are important to our world because they:

- Affirm our human dignity
- Promote the well-being and happiness of the individual
- Serve the common good
- Define our rights and obligations
- Meet the ethical tests of reversibility (in other words, would you want to be treated this way?) and universalizability (would you want all persons to act this way in a similar situation?).

Dr. Thomas Lickona is a developmental psychologist and Professor of Education at the State University of New York at Cortland, where he has done award-winning work in teacher education and currently directs the *Center for the Fourth and Fifth Rs (Respect and Responsibility)*. He is also a member of the advisory board of the Character Counts Coalition. Adapted from www.charactercounts.com

fused to stop the project. He had put a lot of effort into it and he was not going to give up now.

"How do we know how long this other project might take? The other team may not be able to finish it up as planned," Clark said. "As far as the expense you mentioned, you're just making a guess. It might not be as expensive as you say to make the changes . . . if we ever actually need to make them. No, Brenda. I won't change this because of things that *might* happen."

When making a decision, the financial consequences need to be weighed—but only you can decide the weight you will give to an intangible quality like courage.

Clark's position was clear: the information management system would go on. Brenda felt sick. She could only see two choices. One was to go along with Clark even though she believed it would cost the company lots of time and money. Or she could go above Clark and talk to someone else in management. She could let someone else make the decision—but once Clark found out what she had done, her chances of advancement under him would be greatly reduced.

What should Brenda do? She was scared. She wasn't sure she had the courage to go above Clark and risk the consequences. But could she live with herself if she sat back and did nothing?

What would you do in her place?

It takes as much courage to have tried and failed as it does to have tried and succeeded.

—Anne Morrow Lindbergh

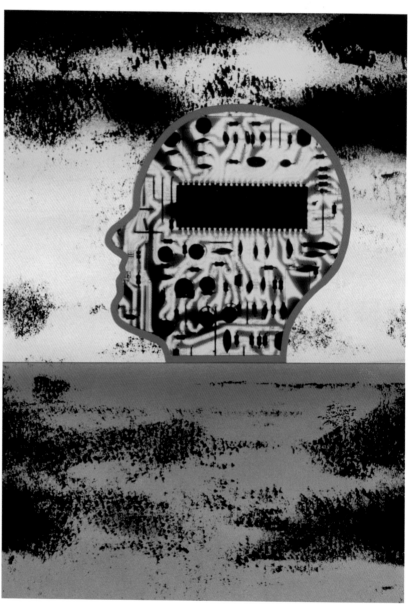

Computer programming gives a new dimension to fantasy and adventure games.

7

SELF-DISCIPLINE AND DILIGENCE

*Good character sometimes
requires sacrifice.*

W ill you ever grow up?" Alan Zalbowitz's mother asked him almost daily when he was in his teens.

"I hope not," Alan always answered.

At 35 years old, Alan was still playing video games. In fact, Alan
wrote game programs for a leading software publisher in Vancouver,
Ontario. Working in the game industry was fun—but also stressful at
times.

For instance, writing an ice hockey game featuring the Erie Otters
had presented Alan with many challenging moments. During the *video
shoots*, team members dressed in specially designed clothing and acted
out the game play. Their special suits had markers attached to them. As
the athlete shot a puck or skated toward the goal, video cameras
recorded every move. Eight cameras could surround one player, pick-
ing up different details and angles of movement. Video shoots were always fun, but for Alan this was one of the best. He loved hockey and the
players were especially animated. They clearly enjoyed hitting pucks,
swinging sticks, and provoking each other. Alan was happy to have
been a part of the shoot.

Then it was Alan's job to turn those moves into computer code.
Writing code that allowed the computer to transform so many actions

into an exciting game took much effort on the part of more than just the programmer.

But now, with the video input and a team of programmers, Alan's job had just begun. With artificial intelligence, they made the players look real on the screen. The players' statistics were also a part of the input, allowing the game players to act and react true to character. The programmers even included whom each player should push and how they would foul each other. As he worked and reworked the project, Alan kept remembering something a friend in college used to say over and over again: "Good coding makes fun, realistic games."

> ### Some Definitions
>
> **Self-discipline** *noun:* Training and control of oneself and one's conduct, usually for personal improvement.
>
> **Diligence** *noun:* Sticking to a task until completion; following through on life's tasks even when they are boring or inconvenient.

Today's computer world touches the world of finances, law enforcement, medicine—and recreation.

Designing computer games may be a fun job—but like any job, it may also at times require long hours of work.

DigiPen School—Where Studying Games Is Work

In 1988 in Vancouver, British Columbia, Claude Comair's classes in 3D computer animation production led to an entire new school for video game programming students. The two-year video game programming diploma course was the first of its kind in North America. Offered in cooperation with Nintendo of America, the program gave students an opportunity to learn exactly what they needed for a career in game programming.

In January 1998, building on the success of the Vancouver campus, DigiPen opened the DigiPen Institute of Technology in Redmond, Washington. DigiPen's newest campus is the first school in the world to offer degree-granting programs for video game programming.

Good coding takes time.

Alan agreed. But he couldn't help adding to himself: *Good coding takes so much time!* So many small bits were needed to create a championship game . . . and their deadline was closing in on them.

As he thought these things, Alan watched one of his team members open the game's beginning.

"I really want to tweak these colors a little," Sondra said. She enlarged the screen until it was filled with a grid of colored boxes. "If I change this orange to blue I think we'll get a little more definition on that emblem on the back of the uniform." She closed the screen and again opened the game. As the player moved across the ice, Alan could see the emblem much better.

"Good graphics. The guys up-

> Self-discipline means saying yes to the right things and no to the wrong things. It means controlling yourself. Self-discipline involves obedience. George Washington's mother was once asked how she raised such a remarkable son. "I taught him to obey," she answered. Following directions and obeying rules are a part of self-discipline.

The answers to life's dilemmas can't always be found in books!

stairs will love it," Alan said. "I wonder if any of them play these games?"

"Who knows," Sondra answered. "I guess all that matters is that somebody plays them. Well, lots of somebodies." She laughed.

Alan now had all the parts of the game together and it was ready to be tested as a whole. The company employed testers, who not only played the game but also looked for ways to make the game mess up. Later that week, Gary Franssen, another programmer on Alan's team, brought the test results.

"Great game," Gary said. "It will be really popular but there's a big 'crash' bug. The game freezes every time I try this one play. Let me show you."

Gary restarted the game on Alan's computer. He moved to the needed screen—and just as he had said, the game froze. Alan had missed this play altogether. He and Gary tried the play a few more times, but they always got the same result: a frozen screen and a new game. This would frustrate players and cause complaints. But Gary was right: except for this one glitch, the game was good.

The project deadline had already passed, but Alan knew he would have until Monday to get the game ready to market. He also knew he had a big weekend planned with his friends. They were going to drive four-wheelers back into the woods to camp, fish, and hike. This was a weekend they had planned for a long time.

Alan was fairly sure he would not have any problems from management if he released the game with this one glitch in the program. Many first versions have just such a problem. In fact, he knew of more than one company that had been accused of purposely releasing a product without fully testing it just so they could get a second version ready to release as soon as possible. But Alan took pride in his work and in the work of his team. He felt the game should warrant a second version not because it had problems, but because it was good and played well, without any "crashes." He hated to miss a weekend in the country—but he really wanted his work to be the best it could be.

When people encounter ethical dilemmas like this one, they need self-discipline. This character trait means you tell yourself what needs

According to the DigiPen Institute of Technology, the advantages of game-oriented productions are:

- Games are graphics-oriented simulations, including two- and three-dimensional based simulations.
- Games can realistically reproduce or simulate natural phenomena and real-life events. Flight simulators are excellent examples of such simulations.
- Games are highly interactive, requiring an elaborate and efficient graphical user interface (GUI). The development of a GUI requires the management of windows, menus, dialog boxes, and hardware resources including keyboards, mice, and display monitors.
- Games react in real time. The implementation of such simulations requires a thorough knowledge of computer hardware and computer languages.
- Games are story-based simulations requiring a plot in which game objects must interact intelligently with each other. Therefore, in order to make games challenging and interesting, students must design and implement good artificial intelligence **algorithms**, which serve as the cognitive processes for the computer-controlled game objects.
- Games can be designed for either a single-player or multiple-player environment. The development of a multiple-player game requires the understanding of subjects such as Computer Networks, TCP/IP, and Internet programming.
- Games are excellent examples of large and complex productions. Teamwork is essential to the successful completion of such productions. Therefore, students are divided into teams and are rigorously trained in object-oriented programming languages, **paradigms**, and software engineering techniques and practices. These collaborative efforts reinforce student ability to work competently within a group while completing projects.

Adapted from the DigiPen Institute of Technology at www.digipen.edu

to be done, even when no one else is giving you orders; you are obedient to your own sense of what is right. Diligence, self-discipline's companion trait, means you keep working until you find success, even when it would be easier or more convenient to simply walk away from a job.

Alan made his decision. "Hey, Sondra, I'm going to be working all weekend to finish up this game. Have you got anything planned? Could you work on a 'crash' problem with me?"

What would you have done in Alan's place?

The first and best victory is to conquer self.

—Plato

You may feel as though professional success is a lonely mountain you climb all by yourself—but you are actually part of an interconnected community.

8

CITIZENSHIP

Sometimes we forget that we each have an important part to play in the community if it is to remain a friendly environment.

Burhan looked at the memo on his desk. Frank Pierson's mother was being operated on tomorrow, a serious surgery at a hospital in a neighboring state. Frank would be away for the next week. The on-call schedule for production support needed to be changed because of Frank's family crisis, and the project manager was asking for volunteers to fill in for Frank while he was away.

Frank was always a team player when they worked on any project. He and Burhan had helped each other out of more than one information or coding problem. Burhan did feel he should help. He knew how close Frank was to his mom and how hard it had been on them both since Frank's dad died last spring.

Burhan loved working on the team and had really enjoyed this project. He had spent numerous nights working in product support, which meant he had already been away from home many evenings. Now, his wife Janna had come down with the flu; that meant tonight he needed to make dinner and take care of the kids. He just didn't think he could fit in product support, not this week.

Putting the memo aside, Burhan began work on his programming project. He would give the project manager his decision before he left

A family is a small community—when as family members we work together to make our home a better place, we are good citizens.

A Definition

Citizenship *noun:* The status of a citizen with its attendant duties, rights, and privileges; working together to make the entire community a better place for everyone.

for home. He felt sorry for Frank . . . but given the circumstances in his own life, Burhan didn't think anyone could expect him to do more than he was already doing.

Later that night, the smell of lasagna filled the kitchen as Burhan walked in the door. Was Janna feeling well enough to cook? He entered the family room, where the children were playing a game and Janna lay on the sofa covered with blankets and surrounded by tissues, orange juice, a humidifier, and a vase of flowers.

"Ruth Weller came over with dinner, dessert, and these flowers about an hour ago," Janna said. "And she says Paula Mitchell is bringing dinner tomorrow night. Isn't that so nice of them?"

"That is really nice." He glanced around at the neat, shining house. "Did Ruth clean up too?"

Just as basketball players cannot play the game all alone, we each depend on the other members of our "team."

Citizenship means that each of us is a necessary part of our community— and we pull together for our common good.

Janna nodded. "Aren't we lucky to have such good friends?"

The dinner was delicious, and as Burhan put dishes into the dishwasher he remembered the memo. His day had been busy, and he had forgotten that he meant to give the project manager his decision before he left work. Now he was happy he hadn't. After he talked things over with Janna, he would give his decision tomorrow.

He still needed to consider Janna's needs. But their friends' example made him feel he wanted to do what he could to help Frank as well. Maybe, he mused, that's the way life ought to be: everyone working together to see that all the bases were covered, both personally and professionally.

This we know, all things are connected.
Like the blood which unites one family, all things are connected.
. . . We did not weave the web of life.
We are merely a strand in it.
Whatever we do to the web, we do to ourselves.
Let us give thanks for the web and the circle that connects us.

—Chief Seattle

The computer programming that created the Internet changed the way we live, connecting our world in a brand new way.

9

CAREER OPPORTUNITIES

*No matter what career you choose, start
now for a lifetime of character.*

Amy Maynard is a computer science major at a state university. She wants to work in programming when she graduates. Amy is also very creative; in her spare time, she makes pieced and appliquéd quilts. Her work is very detailed and everyone who sees her quilts marvels at her precise stitching. Amy loves to solve problems and given a challenge she will work endlessly until it is accomplished.

With most of her fundamental courses behind her, Amy has begun her programming, networking, and database classes, as well as advanced mathematics courses. Recently while looking at the job market predictions, Amy decided to specialize in accounting. Being disciplined and responsible, she feels she will do well in finance. Her advisor has recommended that she seek summer employment in a financial environment and that she should consider an internship her senior year. This specialization will offer her additional opportunities for employment and advancement in her field. But Amy wonders if this area of computer programming will be creative enough for her. She's also considering using her skills in the field of science; forensic sciences particularly fascinate her, and she knows computer programmers in that field have the opportunity to develop programs that help solve crimes.

The computer-programming field is very diverse. From large cor-

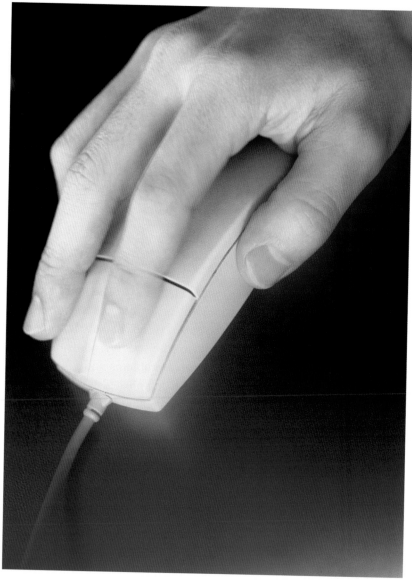

Whether or not you choose a career in computer programming, in today's world, everyone needs some knowledge of computers.

porations to software companies to government employment, programmers are an essential part of the workforce. The largest concentrations of programmers are employed in the computer and data processing industry, and this trend is predicted to continue over the next ten years. Occupations with the firms that write and sell software are among the top employers. But many firms that service other businesses or individuals also hire computer programmers. Engineering, management, telecommunications, and insurance services often employ their own programmers. Many are employed on a temporary or contract basis as independent consultants. Working as an independent programmer benefits the programmer and the company; the programmer uses her expertise, while the contracting firm avoids the expenses of training existing employees or paying her medical and other benefits.

Computer programmers, like Amy, who specialize in business, engineering, or scientific careers may progress to senior positions, such as programmer analysts or computer systems analysts. Systems analysts solve computer problems and help an organization get optimum use from their equipment, personnel, and business processes. They need to work with the software applications and the hardware to make these systems work.

Programmers with an understanding of specific businesses, who

Canadian Computer Programmers

- Approximately 53,100 people were employed in 2000.
- 9% are self-employed.
- 25% are women.
- 92% are employed full-time.
- 44% are employed in business service.
- 14% are employed in manufacturing.
- 13% are employed in finance and insurance.
- 9% are employed in government service.
- 57% are employed in Toronto which is 42% of all occupations.
- Starting hourly wage in March 1999 was $17.19 but the most frequently paid hourly wage was $22.72.

Adapted from the Ontario Job Futures 2000 sites at www.on.hrdcdrhc.gc.ca/english/lmi/eaid/ojf/ojf_home_e.html.

More and more businesses are developing a code of ethics for their employees, including their computer programmers. The General Moral Imperatives from the Association for Computing Machinery say employees must agree to:

1. Contribute to society and human well-being.
2. Avoid harm or negative consequences to others.
3. Be honest and trustworthy.
4. Be fair and take action not to discriminate.
5. Honor property rights, including copyrights and patents.
6. Give proper credit for intellectual property. Specifically, one must not take credit for others' ideas or work.
7. Respect the privacy of others.
8. Honor confidentiality.

have strong technical skills, and who keep up with changing programming languages will be in increased demand. Networking within businesses and the use of client/server and web-based environments mean that programmers who can support data communications, electronic commerce, and Intranet strategies will help businesses move forward in the 21st century. Obtaining vendor or language specific certification provides an edge in most instances. Practical experience, like Amy's summer employment and internship, increases job opportunities.

Although education provides one avenue to employment, good character is another. Employers look for the best employee they can get to fill a position—and the best candidate will always be someone who combines expertise and character.

So if you want to be a computer programmer, remember: practicing character is just as important as practicing code-writing skills. Start now. Be the person you want to be!

Association for Computing Machinery

Founded in 1947, ACM is the world's first educational and scientific computing society. The ACM has written a Code of Ethics and Professional Conduct that has at its basis a commitment to ethical professional conduct. The code consists of 24 statements of personal commitment. Fundamental ethical considerations are outlined and are intended as a basis for ethical decision making, emphasizing that ethical principles, which apply to computer ethics, are derived from more general ethical principles.

The world of computer programming spans the globe.

Hiring special needs persons happens within the computer programming field. Mark Dodd is blind, but he has not allowed his disability to keep him from pursuing his career. As a computer programmer, he maintains the current programs, designs new systems for contracting officers, and creates web sites. Through the use of assistive technology, Mark has been able to advance from his position as a computer instructor at a local community rehabilitation program to his current position at a bank.

Opening up career opportunities within computer programming to the disabled allows another part of the job force to share in the feelings of self-worth, courage, and respect that come from being employed. With increased technology and assisted services, more jobs should be available in the future to those with disabilities.

Adapted from http://www.nish.org/news/wp1097-3.html.

It takes courage to grow up and turn out to be who you really are.

—*e.e. cummings*

FURTHER READING

Bennett, William J. *The Book of Virtues for Young People.* New York: Simon & Schuster for Young Readers, 1997.

Josephson, Michael S. and Wes Hanson, editors. *The Power of Character.* San Francisco: Jossey-Bass, 1998.

Kidder, Rushworth M. *How Good People Make Tough Choices.* New York: Simon & Schuster, 1995.

Wang, Wallace. *Beginning Programming for Dummies.* California: IDG Books Worldwide, Inc., 1999.

For More Information

C++ Tutorial - Lesson 1: A First Program
http://cplus.about.com/library/weekly/aa020502a.htm

Character Education Network
www.charactered.net

Focus on Java
http://java.about.com/index.htm?iam=dpile&terms=computer+programming

Josephson Institute of Ethics
www.josephsoninstitute.org

Webopedia
www.webopedia.com

GLOSSARY

Automate To computerize.

BASIC An acronym for Beginner's All-purpose Symbolic Instruction Code. It's a simplified language used for programming a computer.

Clone Something identical to the original model.

COBOL An acronym for common business oriented language. COBOL is the second-oldest programming language and is very wordy. When writing a program using COBOL, the instructions are long because everything is written down. This makes it an easy program to understand but can be exasperating for those writing the code.

Forensic When scientific knowledge is used to deal with legal issues, particularly crimes.

Hack To gain access to computer programs illegally.

Kernel The core code or module of the operating system. Although the system is composed of other modules, the kernel loads first and remains in the memory during memory management, task management, and disk management.

Operating system Manages the computer by running the application programs. Application programs are written for specific operating systems and cannot be used interchangeably. Operating systems work by recognizing input from the keyboard, sending information to the computer screen, keeping track of files on the hard drive, and guiding the functions of printers, scanners, and other peripheral devices.

Paradigms Patterns or frameworks.

Programming language The "language" or set of symbols understood by the computer that allows a programmer to write new functions for the computer.

PROLOG Short for programming logic. It is a language based on logical formulas. Instead of traditionally performing a sequence of commands, PROLOG's programs consist of a list of facts and rules. It is used for artificial intelligence applications.

Viruses Computer programs that are designed to spread from computer to computer by producing copies of themselves and inserting them into other programs; viruses are usually malicious and expensive pranks that can cause computers to lose data or essential programming.

INDEX

algorithms 69
Andreesen, Mark 10
applications programmers 7
artificial intelligence 64, 69
assistive technology 84
Association for Computing Machinery
    (ACM) 83

BASIC 5, 10

Cerf, Vinton 9
character 1–3, 5, 6, 12, 16, 30, 51, 52, 59,
    63, 79, 82
cheating 22
Chief Seattle 77
citizenship 74
COBOL 7
code analyzers 33
compassion 28
computers, as investigative tool 49
confidential information 8
core values 10
courage 56
"crashes" 68, 70

DigiPen 65, 69
diligence 64, 66

educational requirements 6
ethical dilemma 29–30, 57, 68
ethics 21, 82, 83

fairness 38
first computer 8

hacking 9

independent consultants 81
integrity 18, 20, 23, 25

Jefferson, Thomas 23
justice 38, 39

Kahn, Robert 9
kernel 5

Linux 5

moral responsibilities 50

Netscape communications 10

Olympic creed 58
operating system 5

paradigms 69
Plato 71
principles of good character 6
programming language 7
Prolog 7

respect 28
responsibility 46, 47
Roosevelt, Eleanor 57

SchoolNet GrassRoots National
    Campaign 13
self-discipline 64, 66, 70
software development 8

Thomas, Clarence 12
Torvalds, Linus 5–7
Transmission Control Protocol/Internet
    Protocol (TCP/IP) 9

viruses 9

BIOGRAPHIES

Sherry Bonnice lives in a log cabin on a dirt road in Montrose, Pennsylvania, with her husband, teenage daughter, five dogs, and 25 rabbits. She loves homeschooling her daughter, reading, and making quilts. Sherry has spent the last two years coediting three quilt magazines and writing a quilt book. Writing books for children and young people has been her dream.

Cheryl Gholar is a Community and Economic Development Educator with the University of Illinois Extension. She has a Ph.D. in Educational Leadership and Policy Studies from Loyola University, and she has more than 20 years of experience with the Chicago Public Schools as a teacher, counselor, guidance coordinator, and administrator. Recognized for her expertise in the field of character education, Dr. Gholar assisted in developing the K–12 Character Education Curriculum for the Chicago Public Schools, and she is a five-year participant in the White House Conference on Character Building for a Democratic and Civil Society. The recipient of numerous awards, she is also the author of *Beyond Rhetoric and Rainbows: A Journey to the Place Where Learning Lives.*

Ernestine G. Riggs is an Assistant Professor at Loyola University Chicago and a Senior Program Consultant for the North Central Regional Educational Laboratory. She has a Ph.D. in Educational Leadership and Policy Studies from Loyola University, and she has been involved in the field of education for more than 35 years. An advocate of teaching the whole child, she is a frequent presenter at district and national conferences; she also serves as a consultant for several state boards of education. Dr. Riggs has received many citations, including an award from the United States Department of Defense Overseas Schools for Outstanding Elementary Teacher of America.